DESTROYING DESTRUCTIVE DREAMS

SAMUEL A. WRIGHT

Unless otherwise indicated, all scripture quotations are taken from the King James Version of the Holy Bible.

Scripture quotations marked NKJV are from the Holy Bible, New King James Version.

Destroying Destructive Dreams
- Samuel A. Wright

Copyright © 2010 Samuel A. Wright

ISBN: 978-978-50151-3-3

Redeeming Hope Christian Centre
P. O. Box 11966, Ikeja, Lagos, Nigeria
Alpha1_ministries@yahoo.com
www.redeeminghopechristiancenter.org

Contents

## CHAPTER ONE

What Does It Mean To Dream?

The Longman Dictionary of contemporary English defines dream as a series of thoughts, images and feelings that are experienced when asleep. It also described dream as a state of mind in which you do not notice or pay attention to things around you.

It is therefore very pertinent to define dream in this context as, "spiritual information or messages transmitted from the spiritual world to our inner beings at a time when we are unconscious".

Very often, such information or messages related in dreams appear in form of parables. They come in thoughts, pictorial view, images or feelings.

Essentially, dream take place in the subconscious realm, and it is mainly an exercise of the soul.

Man is a three in one personality. He is a spirit; he has a soul and lives in a body.

The soul is usually actively involved in dreams. Dreams are a product of the activities of man's brain or soul.

During a dream, a person watches or takes part in activities and events. These events in dream may look very imaginary but they are undoubtedly connected to the life experience of the dreamer.

The events in dreams always look very real to the dreamer, and occasionally may be very fearful.

Such dreams which are nightmares could be very frightening, irritating, annoying, strange and unpleasant.

While some dreams are associated with annoyance, fear, anger, annoyance, etc. Some, however, elicit pleasure and good feelings.

Many people often forget their dreams. Only a few people practically recall the totality of their dreams.

We sometimes remember only bits and pieces of our dreams, which occasionally enable us to paint or have a good picture or message of the dream. Sometimes we remember our dreams while we are just trying to wake up from sleep. But it is only very few people that can actually recall their dreams once they are fully awake and get involved in other daily activities at the same time.

However, there are times when your dream becomes very clear to you as a living picture.

Suggested Prayers:

1.   Empower my dream life for absolute transformation, in Jesus' name.

2.   I shall not be a prey, in Jesus' name.

3.   My dream shall speak and not die in Jesus' name.

4.   I surround my dream life with the blood of Jesus.

5.   I secure my dream life with the power of the Holy Ghost.

6.   My dream life will affect my physical life positively, in Jesus' name.

7.   I should not be a captive of evil dreams in Jesus' name.

8.   Your plan for me oh Lord shall not be vandalized in the dream in Jesus' name.

CHAPTER TWO

Facts About Dreams

Dreams and dreaming is a part of life. But for us to appreciate the importance of our dreams, we need to understand the content of what dream entails.

Dreams can come in coded form or parables therefore it is subject to misconception, misinterpretation and manipulations.

We have said that dream is a means through which God communicates to people; but Satan can also use it against man.

Please note that dream usually have the following traits and common truths:

- God uses dreams for us while Satan uses dreams against man

- When good dreams comes, you need to pray for the fulfillment and when bad dream come, pray against it and use the blood of Jesus to cancel it.

- Dreams can be remembered or forgotten. Some people only remember their dreams partially

- The Holy spirit can help bring your dreams into remembrance, if you ask Him - John 14:26"

- Dreams can indicate progress or stagnation and it therefore affects destines

- Dreams can lead a man to major breakthroughs or breakdown in his life

- God can terminate a long term stagnation, sickness or failure or evil experiences through dreams

- Dream are mysterious

- The devil, demon and witchcraft powers can intrude the dream life of a man

- Dreams are God's channel of safely passing information across to man, which he may not find in daily worship, devotion in prayers or in the Bible

- One can dream in the day, noon or night

- Dreams are generally not taken serious by many until they begin to be sign   of the fulfillment of such dreams

- Many people are ignorant of certain destiny changing dreams that could transform their lives (Gen 28:16)

- Dreams and visions are Gods programs or agenda for the end time church, to advance the destiny of man, and to give directions (Joel 2:28)

Indeed there are many facts about dreams too numerous to discuss here. But highlighted below are a few more inherent facts we would find in dreams, which would give us a better understand of dreams:

1.   Science cannot interpret dreams or analyse your dreams. Dreams are spiritual activities played out in the soulish realm

2.   Dreams are not just fairy tales or meaningless thoughts. They have meanings relevant to the life of the dreamer.

3.   In some dreams the dreamer takes part in the story. He may be a major player in the drama, while in others, the dreamer watches as the story unfolds.

4.   On several occasion, the dreamer cannot control the event or happenings in the dreams. It is like watching a movie you have no control over.

5.   Most dreams contain a lot of strange elements or illogical events that may not happen in real life, but they are graphically presented in the dream life.

6.   In some cases, the dreamer is aware of the fact that he is in a dream world or another realm.

7.   Dreams involve the use of sense organ, therefore people see, hear, smell, touch and taste in dreams.

8.   The unexpected takes place in dreams. It is a fantasy world; a strange one!

9.   Dreams usually have information to pass across to the dreamer; and it also convey very reliable messages.

10.   Dreams may include events, sights, discussions and / or feelings that the dreamer had experienced or participated in during hours preceding sleep.

11.   Dreams may come as a result of deep wishes and fears orchestrated by the dreamer.

12   Psychologists and Social Scientists as far back as 1890's in the time of Sigmund Freud, an Austrian physician, suggested that dreams are a fulfilment of the wishes of the dreamer, and that dreams are always very meaningful. Dreams therefore may appear scattered and meaningless, but it does have deep meanings.

13.   Dreams can come in parables or coded messages. This is why many dreams seem strange, queer and mysterious to many people.

14.   The enemy / devil can distort the dream life of an individual. Dream is a veritable means through which the powers of darkness have access to people's destiny and thereby afflict them.

Suggested Prayers:

1.   I shall prevail in my dream life, in Jesus' name.

2.   My dream life shall not die, in Jesus' name

3.   Evil altars against my dream life, scatter by thunder, in Jesus' name.

4.   Wherever evil hands are joined together against me, over my dream life, be broken to pieces, in Jesus' name.

5.   Evil voice calling me in the dream be silenced in Jesus' name.

6.   Killer of dreams you will not kill my dream in, Jesus' name.

7.   Any filthy dream introduced into my life, die in Jesus' name.

8.   Vindicate me oh Lord through my dreams, in Jesus' name

9.   Let my dream life be totally free from pollution in Jesus' name.

10.   I shall arise and shine, in Jesus' name

CHAPTER THREE

Sources of Dreams

Basically, there are three sources through which dreams can come to a person. There are dreams from God; dreams from Satan; and there are dreams emanating from man himself.

1.   Dreams From God
Since times of old, God has been speaking to mankind through several media, and dreams are one of such means.

God relates information and gives instruction and directives to His people through dreams. Indeed, many of our dreams are actual communication with our Creator. This is why we must not disregard any dream.

2.   Dreams From Satan

The devil also initiates dreams in the minds of people when they sleep.

Usually, dreams from Satan cause fear; they bring discouragement; promote feelings of hopelessness and they often lead to confusion and sorrow or bitterness in their wake.

3.   Dreams From Man

As long as man lives in this world, his mind and living would continually be shaped and determined by what is on this earth. This is why majority of the dreams people dream are from the human mind and his every day encounter with the world, its elements and with other people or happenings.

> *"For a dream comes through much activity, And a fool's voice is known by his many words.*
> *[7] For in the multitude of dreams and many words there is also vanity"*
> *(Eccl 5: 3 &7, NKJV)*

Who Can Dream?

If dreams come from man, what categories of people dream dreams? Can just any one have dream experience?

Yes. Everyone that has a living soul can and should dream. This is what Bible says concerning God's mind the issue of dreams,

> *"And it shall come to pass afterward, that I will pour out my spirit upon all flesh; and your sons and your daughters shall prophesy, your old men shall dream dreams, your young men shall see vision"*
> *(Joel 2:28, NKJV)*

What the Bible is saying here is:

- As people had visions and dreams in ancient times, so will they now have clearer revelations in contemporary times

- People of all ages and ranks would dream, not just a privileged few. This is what, "sons, daughters, old and young" means.

Furthermore, this means that the knowledge of God and His purpose or will shall boom among all ranks, sexes and ages in the Messiah's days, and even surpass what was previously encountered by man.

The simple and clear meaning of this is that, all humans, whether black or white; young or old; children or adults; educated or illiterate; rich or poor; masters or servants; have the ability to dream.

It is even a dangerous thing for a person not to dream at all.

Suggested Prayers:

1.   Any attack on my dream life shall die, in Jesus' name.

2.   Evil arrow in my dream shall not prosper against me, in Jesus' name.

3.   I refuse to be victimised in my dream, in Jesus' name.

4.   Oh Lord, scatter those who are using my dream life against me, in Jesus' name.

5.   Night radars will not prevail over my dream life, in Jesus' name

6.   The vision, information and revelation my life needs for advancement, appear in my dream now, in Jesus' name.

7.   Dreams of poverty, rejection, tragedy, failure, oppressor, frustration, infirmity, be cancelled by the blood of Jesus

8.   Witchcraft foundation in my family, be dismantled, in Jesus' name.

9.   Every power assigned to curse my destiny, begin to bless my destiny, in Jesus' name.

10.   My Father, make my enemies stepping stones for my greatness, in Jesus' name.

## CHAPTER FOUR

7 Factors That Influence Dreams

There are a few factors that influences our dream life, which determines the kind of dreams we have and how they affect our lives.

It is therefore very important that we carefully take note of these factors and consider how they affect us or relate to us.

1.   Association:

The company we keep influences our dream life.

Those who go about partying and are always walking about in the night, when so many strange activities take place, are prone to having destructive dreams.

Those who watch horror films and sexually perverted films are not far from destruction. Their dream would be invaded by evil and unpleasant occurrences.

## 2.	Environment:

The environment where we live goes a long way to influence our dream life.

Some environments are cursed. Some houses are dedicated to idols and strange gods. Those who live in such houses and neighborhood where occultic practices are common, or residences where village or community masquerades reside are exposed to destructive dreams and their evils.

## 3.	Sickness, Worry and Anxiety:

These physical and emotional conditions can also influence the dream life of a man.

Very often, when a person is attacked by malaria in Africa, the dream changes to nightmares.

## 4.	Your Past:

Our past is not a sleeping dog. It reappears regularly.

Those who have or live lose sexual lives, or those who indulge in occultic practices, or entrenched in deep cultural or traditional practices will always experience high demonic opposition in their dream.

5.   Curses and Evil Covenant:

People who are under a curse and satanic destructive covenants are regular candidates or victims of bad and evil dreams.

6.   Your Relationship with God:

This is by far, the greatest influence of a man's dream. But the question is, what is your relationship with God?

Is your life clean and pleasing to God? Does He approve of your ways?

The Bible says,

"Unto the pure all things are pure: but unto them that are defiled and unbelieving is nothing pure; but even their mind and conscience is defiled."
(Titus 1:15)

The relationship you have with God can influence your dream life.

If the mind is contaminated with impure and unholy images and ideas, and the conscience is defiled with the guilt of sins already committed against God, then it is certain that you would not have peace of mind or a clear heart to receive good vision or dream good dreams, because the enemy takes over whatsoever heart that is not of God.

If you live a life of purity, revelations through vision and dreams would be a regular channel or way of receiving the leading of Holy spirit. This would be daily occurrence instead of nightmares.

## 7.	God's plan for your life:

The plans and purpose of God for your life goes a long way to determine the kind of dream you will have; because severally, He would reveal His mind to you through dreams.

> *" For I know the thoughts that I think toward you, says the LORD, thoughts of peace and not of evil, to give you a future and a hope"*
> *(Jer 29: 11, NKJV)*

If the mind of God towards us is of good and peace, we would hear from Him in our dreams. He would talk to us, guide us and comfort us.

This was what happened to Joseph, the husband of Mary, the mother of Jesus.

> *"But while he thought on these things, behold, the angel of the Lord appeared unto him in a dream, saying, Joseph, thou son of David, fear not to take unto thee Mary thy wife: for that which is conceived in her is of the Holy Ghost. (Matt 1: 20)*

Dreams will bring the appearance of Angels to help you walk in the direction of the purpose of God for your life.

> *"For God may speak in one way, or in another, yet man does not perceive it.*
> *[15] In a dream, in a vision of the night, When deep sleep falls upon men, While slumbering on their beds,*
> *[16] Then He opens the ears of men, and seals their instruction.*
> *[17] In order to turn man from his deed, and conceal pride from man,*
> *[18] He keeps back his soul from the Pit, and his life from perishing by the sword"*

Suggested Prayers:

1.   My Father, let destiny changing dreams begin to manifest in my life today, in Jesus' name.

2.   Oh Lord, appear in my dream and confound any enemy interfering with my life, in Jesus' name.

3.   Every Satanic and witchcraft appearance in my dream, end now, in Jesus' name

4.   Every power assigned against the fulfillment of my dream and vision be frustrated, in Jesus' name.

5.   Every good vision and dream that people have seen concerning my life shall come to pass, in Jesus' name.

6.   Power that delay fulfillment of good dreams in my life, fail in Jesus' name.

7.   All my good dream manifest by fire, in Jesus' name.

8.   Household powers sponsoring failure at the edge of my breakthrough, fail in Jesus' name.

9.   Every coffin prepared for me in the dream catch fire, in Jesus' name.

10.   Satanic dream, be converted to heavenly visions, in Jesus' name.

## CHAPTER FIVE

Biblical Foundation, Purpose & Importance of Dreams

If it is true that everyone can dream, does it mean there is Bible foundation for dreams? Does the Bible support dreams? And what lessons can we learn from these biblical examples?

According to The Strongest Strong's Exhaustive Concordance of The Bible, the word "dreams" appear about seventy-four times in the Bible, while "dreamed" appeared twenty times.

The word "dreamer" appeared four times; "dreamers" two times; "dreamt" two times; and dream twenty-one times.

We can therefore conclude that the word dream is referred to in more than 100 places in the Bible. In other words, men in Bible days dreamt just as men are dreaming today.

Indeed God has been using and still uses dreams to communicate with man on planet earth.

In most cases, dream reveals the voice of God; exposes the condition of the heart of men; and discloses the wicked plans of the devil- calling the destiny of man.

It is unfortunate that many of us today are too busy in the day, and modern technology has made our environment rather noisy and cluttered, and God cannot get to talk with us in the day. Because of this, dream has become the means by which God communicate with men.

Truly, anyone who does not dream needs to pray very well, because if you don't dream at all, a fundamental means of communication is closed to you, since there are many lessons to learn from dreams just as there are information you can glean from dreams.

Lessons & Importance of Dreams:

1.   It reveals the secret of a man's destiny (Joseph: Gen 37-50)

Joseph the son of Jacob learnt from his dreams what the purpose of God for his life was. And it was these dreams that kept him in the face of challenges, slavery, temptations, false accusations and imprisonment.

"Now Joseph had a dream, and he told it to his brothers; and they hated him even more.

6 So he said to them, "Please hear this dream which I have dreamed:

7 "There we were, binding sheaves in the field. Then behold, my sheaf arose and also stood upright; and indeed your sheaves stood all around and bowed down to my sheaf."

8 And his brothers said to him, "Shall you indeed reign over us? Or shall you indeed have dominion over us?" So they hated him even more for his dreams and for his words.

9 Then he dreamed still another dream and told it to his brothers, and said, "Look, I have dreamed another dream. And this time, the sun, the moon, and the eleven stars bowed down to me."

10 So he told it to his father and his brothers; and his father rebuked him and said to him, "What is this dream that you have dreamed? Shall your mother and I and your brothers indeed come to bow down to the earth before you?"
(Gen 37: 5-10)

Joseph suffered emotionally, psychologically, and physically when he was sold by his own brothers.

Such rejection can break the spirit of any man. But the dream of the young Joseph kept him going; it guided him on the path of righteousness, away from lust and away from revenge.

The Bible says in Psalm 105:19 *"Until the time that his word came: the word of the LORD tried him"*.

It is indeed true that when a man knows what his destiny is, he can give anything to achieve it. And note too that if anybody or situation can make you go back on your dream, then it was not originally yours.

In the end, God's secret plan in the life of Joseph after all the drama of slavery, false accusation and eventual rise to prominence was revealed even to his brother and family. See what the Bible says: *"When Joseph's brothers saw that their father was dead, they said, "Perhaps Joseph will hate us, and may actually repay us for all the evil which we did to him" (Gen 50: 15)*

"Joseph said to them, "Do not be afraid, for am I in the place of God?
[20] "But as for you, you meant evil against me; but God meant it for good, in order to bring it about as it is this day, to save many people alive.
[21] "Now therefore, do not be afraid; I will provide for you and your little ones." And he comforted them and spoke kindly to them" (Gen 50: 19-21)

This is what understanding your purpose can do to a man!

2. Dreams Are For Foretelling Future Happenings (Pharaoh's Dreams: Gen 41):

God can use dreams to prophetically tell us what He wants to do concerning a person, family or nation.

God used Pharaoh's dream to show to him that both plenty and want shall come out of Egypt.

> *"Then it came to pass, at the end of two full years, that Pharaoh had a dream; and behold, he stood by the river.*
> *2 Suddenly there came up out of the river seven cows, fine looking and fat; and they fed in the meadow.*
> *3 Then behold, seven other cows came up after them out of the river, ugly and gaunt, and stood by the other cows on the bank of the river.*
> *4 And the ugly and gaunt cows ate up the seven fine looking and fat cows. So Pharaoh awoke.*
> *5 He slept and dreamed a second time; and suddenly seven heads of grain came up on one stalk, plump and good.*
> *6 Then behold, seven thin heads, blighted by the east wind, sprang up after them.*

> *⁷ And the seven thin heads devoured the seven plump and full heads. So Pharaoh awoke, and indeed, it was a dream.*
>
> *⁸ Now it came to pass in the morning that his spirit was troubled, and he sent and called for all the magicians of Egypt and all its wise men. And Pharaoh told them his dreams, but there was no one who could interpret them for Pharaoh"*
> *(Gen 41:1-8)*

God divinely used this dream to position Joseph whom He had revealed His purpose to, as one of the leaders of Egypt, in order to sustain His people in the impending famine or economic melt-down.

Even though there was famine, see what Joseph said to his brothers about how God used providence to do for Israel through Joseph and Pharaoh's dream,

> *"But as for you, you meant evil against me; but God meant it for good, in order to bring it about as it is this day, <u>to save many people alive.</u>*
> *²¹ "Now therefore, do not be afraid; <u>I will provide for you and your little ones</u>." And he comforted them and spoke kindly to them.*
> *²² So Joseph dwelt in Egypt, he and his father's household. And Joseph lived one hundred and ten years"* *(Gen 50: 20-22)*

3.   Dreams Are For Direction And For Warning
(Daniel and Nebuchadnezzar's Dream: Daniel 4:1-37):

Many a times, the Lord would show to us the paths He wants us to follow or what to do. He warns us with signs through our dreams.

But many people disregard such vital leading of God, either through ignorance or wilful disobedience.

This was the case of King Nebuchadnezzar. God showed him in a dream how He wanted to deal with the king and strip him of his glory because he was proud.

Hear the king:

> *"I Nebuchadnezzar was at rest in mine house, and flourishing in my palace:*
> *[5] I saw a dream which made me afraid, and the thoughts upon my bed and the visions of my head troubled me" (Dan 4: 4-5)*

But did the king change his attitude when he discovered the way to avert God's judgement communicated to him through his dream?

No, he did not. He even disregarded the advice of Daniel concerning the dream.

Daniel advised the king thus,

The king did not heed the warning of the dream, and God punished him as He had said. King Nebuchadnezzar became mad and he was driven away by his people and he ended up eating grass like a cow for seven years.

In the case of Joseph, the husband of Mary, the mother of Jesus, he thought it wise to quietly break his proposed marriage to Mary when he discovered that she was pregnant.

Can a virgin become pregnant? That was an unthinkable proposition, and the man Joseph wanted to do what he thought was honourable, that is, let Mary go, without he making any formal complaints to the Jewish authorities.

But for him not to go against the plan of God, the Lord spoke to him concerning Mary and her unborn child in a dream.

> *"But while he thought on these things, behold, the angel of the Lord appeared unto him in a dream, saying, Joseph, thou son of David, fear not to take unto thee Mary thy wife: for that which is conceived in her is of the Holy Ghost (Matt 1:20)*

4. **Dreams Are For Protection** (Joseph, the father of Jesus)

When Jesus was born, the enemy wanted to frustrate God's plan of redemption for mankind by killing the baby, Jesus. But God spoke again to Joseph through a dream to go hide the child in a foreign land.

> *"...Behold, the angel of the Lord appeareth to Joseph in a dream, saying, Arise, and take the young child and his mother, and flee into Egypt, and be thou there until I bring thee word: for Herod will seek the young child to destroy him" (Matt 2:13)*

OTHER PURPOSES & TYPES OF DREAMS

1. **Instructional Dreams** (Gen 30)

Laban cheated Jacob, but God gave Jacob divine instruction and ideas in a dream on what he needed to do to withstand the deceit of Laban.

God often give instructions in the dream concerning what steps to take to put an end to satanic delays, to avert their evils and how to move forward in life.

This kind of dream goes a long way to help man achieve the purpose of God for his life and walk out of oppression, slavery, servant hood, bondage, and break the covenant of hard labour.

## 2.	Warning Dream

God is Alpha and Omega. He declares the end of every matter from the beginning thereof.

When Jesus was born "Matt 2:13" records that King Herod was ready to kill the baby Jesus. But God came in a dream to warn Joseph, the father of Jesus of the impending danger.

The wise men were also warned in the dream that they must not return to king herod on their way back to their country (Matt 2:12)

## 3.	Restoration Dream

Many of us have lost precious things through dreams. But God is able and willing to restore all that the enemy has stolen from us, including the good things we lost through our own carelessness.

In **Gen 40:6-13,** the butler who was with Joseph in prison had a restoration dream and the fulfillment of the dream came in **Gen 40:21-22.**

May the lord restore all you have ever lost in life, in Jesus' name.

4.   Revelational Dreams (Acts 27 :22-26)

God use dreams to give insight into the happenings in the nearest past or distant future.

Dreams come when God is ready to reveal hidden secrets. This is to demonstrate the power of God who alone can reveal secrets. It is also to frustrate all the efforts of the wicked and destructive powers assigned against our destiny.

Revelational dreams often expose the secret of the wicked ones.

"He reveals deep and secret things; He knows what is in the darkness, And light dwells with Him" (Dan 2:22)

Paul was well informed about what was to ultimately happen to him as he undertook his journey to Jerusalem.

5.   Dream of Assurance (Gen 46:1-4)

God spoke to Jacob in a night vision to assure him of his continuous backup. The presence of God can be granted in a dream or vision. Very often this is to remove every form of fear.

In **Gen 28:15** God also assured Jacob of divine protection in a dream.

In **2 Chron 1:7** God appeared to Solomon in a night dream and promised to grant whatever he requested for, after he had offered a great sacrifice.

6.   Dreams Foretelling The Future

Dreams are also designed to foretell the future. God revealed His future plans for the life and destiny of Joseph in coded messages in his dreams **(Gen 37:5-7)**

When Joseph informed his family members, they hated and envy him because of these dreams. This is a lesson for us here is. It is not all dreams that we must tell to others.

Some dreams and visions of life are spiritually and specifically meant to give information and to stir or inspire positive prayers. This is necessary if we must witness the fulfillment of such dreams and to prevent the gang up of the powers of darkness against such dreams.

7.   Healing Dreams

A sister once shared a dream she had with me. She dreamt that an elderly minister of the gospel in Nigeria appeared to her and laid hands on her legs and she received her healing.

A woman also had a dream and saw doctors carry out operation on her. Immediately after, her affliction of eleven years came to an end.

8.   Fruitful Dreams

Dreams can announce the arrival of destiny children, as we find in the case of Joseph concerning the birth of Jesus and Mary's pregnancy (Mtt 1:20-21)

9. Promises In Dreams

The promises of God can also come through dreams.

God promised Jacob in a dream that he shall be blessed, and that he shall posses his possessions in the land of the living (**Gen 28:12-16**)

In summary, the importance and purpose of dream amongst many others include:

- God gives direction to people's life through dreams
- Dreams are for instruction, guidance, and correction.
- Dreams reveal the plan and purpose of God for your life.
- Significant things or major event of life can be communicated through dreams.
- Dreams help the dreamer to understand himself better.
- Dreams communicate the mind of God to man.
- Information about the past, present and future concerning a man's life can be passed through dreams (Job 33: 14-18)
- God uses dreams to encourage and comfort the soul of man, by divinely getting involved in his affairs.
- The grace and gifts of God can be imparted through dream as in the case of Solomon (I kings 3:5)
- Covenants can be enacted in dreams. As God did with Abraham (Gen 15)

Dreams have biblical foundation, and the purpose of dream is indeed very numerous. Our challenge is, how do we respond to our dreams?

I pray that from henceforth, you shall hear God's voice to shape your destiny through your dreams. May you hear His teaching voice. May His plans of protection become clearer to you even in your dreams, in Jesus' name.

Suggested Prayers:

1.   That power that disgraced Goliath, that killed Herod, that sank Pharaoh, arise and disgrace the stubborn problems of my life, in Jesus' name.

2.   Anointing to fulfil my divine agenda fall on me now, in Jesus' name.

3.   Ancestral burden to my greatness, be dismantled, in Jesus' name.

4.   Evil crowd assigned to mock my destiny, be disgraced, in Jesus' name.

5.   Every bitter river programmed to flow into my life, dry up, in Jesus' name.

6.   Let shame and reproach cover my enemies and oppressors, in Jesus' name.

7.   Powers that sponsors bad dreams, be paralyzed, in Jesus' name.

8.   Imagination of the wicked against my life be cancelled, in Jesus' name.

9.   Wickedness of the wicked, rest upon their heads, in Jesus' name.

10.   Every arrow, gunshots fired into my life in the dream, return to sender, in Jesus' name.

## CHAPTER SIX

Interpreting Your Dreams

It is very important to stress here that dreams are very symbolic. They carry a lot of meaning that can shape or affect your life and destiny.

Therefore, caution must be taken in interpreting and acting on dreams.

We should be cautious of what we accept as interpretation of our dreams.

A few years back, I had a dream which clearly was a destructive dream; but my situation became worsened because of the people I shared the dreams with.

And for about 4 years I was tossed up and down from one prayer mountain to another with different kind of interpretations coming from different kinds of people. Yet My life became more miserable until I found divine solution to my problem.

In that particular dream, I dream that I was placed in a coffin and about to be buried. As I lied down in the coffin, I soon realized that my would be executors were nailing the coffin, and in desperation to come out, I used my head to repeatedly hit the door of the coffin to force it open.

It was at this moment I woke up. But immediately I tried to stand, I discovered that something terrible and strange had happened. Water was trickling out of my mouth, and I could no longer stand. The next thing I discovered was that I woke up three days later in the hospital with drips passed all over me.

And this was the beginning of my travails. May you not wake up as a victim of your enemies, in Jesus name!

Because of the strange illness that resulted from that dream, I was carried from place to place seeking help for fours years. And several of the interpretation given by pastors and ministers of God to my dream was that death was imminent because so many people who had such dreams died.

But was this really true? Thank God that all those interpretations were contrary to the plan of God for my live. And to the glory of God, I am alive today, hale and hearty.

It is on this note that I emphatically declare that precise or correct interpretation of any dream in life can only come from God. This truth is what Joseph made the officers of Pharaoh to understand and appreciate.

> *"And they said unto him, We have dreamed a dream, and there is no interpreter of it. And Joseph said unto them, Do not interpretations belong to God? tell me them, I pray you" (Gen 40:8)*

Dreams do not belong to the realm of the physical; it therefore requires the non-physical to explain or understand it. This is where the Spirit of God takes centre stage.

The Spirit of God is omniscient. He knows all things; and can therefore interpret dreams. This is why it takes a man who has the Spirit of God to correctly interpret dreams.

The Bible says, Daniel could interpret dreams, because, *"... God gave them knowledge and skill in all learning and wisdom: and Daniel had understanding in all visions and dreams" (Dan 1:17)*

> *"Inasmuch as an excellent spirit, knowledge, understanding, interpreting dreams, solving riddles, and explaining enigmas were found in this Daniel, whom the king named Belteshazzar, now let Daniel be called, and he will give the interpretation" (Dan 5: 12, NKJV)*

I earnestly want to point out here too, THAT DREAMS CANNOT BE INTERPRETED MECHANICALLY OR IN A PREPARED FORMAT OR BOOK THAT IS CONSULTED WHEN WE DREAM.

To do this is simply to reduce dream to science or mathematics where one plus one equals two!

Even though many scientist and inventors attest to the fact that most of their discoveries come through dreams, nevertheless, Science can never and must not be used to interpret dreams.

The fact that a lady had a dream where she saw herself walking on the street with a brother and they both held hands does not indicate that God has approved their marriage plans.

I believe that if Joseph, the Dreamer, lived in our time, and comes to say, *"I have dreamed another dream. And this time, the sun, the moon, and the eleven stars bowed down to me" (Gen 37:9),* many of us would say he needs deliverance, because a lot of people associates the moon and other elemental forces with the powers of darkness.

Many people have assumed positions or the office of dream interpretation using logic, manipulation, guile and mechanically manufactured principles and theories to tell what is not.

"It happened to Mr. A when he had that kind of dream, therefore it must happen to you!"

But, that Philip saw a coffin in his dream and died does not mean if Michael sees one then he mus tautomatically die.

Each dream has its own meaning based on what the Holy Spirit is passing across to you or wants you to know or do.

However, there are simple basic things you must understand about dreams which would help in understanding them:

- Note that the beginning and the end of a dream are very important in any attempt to interpret our dreams.

- Dreams from God do not bring fear of any kind.

- Repetition of any dream signifies the importance and the need for   urgent prayer and attention.

Suggested Generally Accepted Meanings / Interpretation To Dream

Undoubtedly, there are destructive dreams from the pit of hell. Satan uses dream to attack the destiny and life of men and women from all walks of life.

Pastors and counselors will agree with me that a larger percentage of the people we attend to these days in church often come to share one dream or the other they had and how it affects their lives.

There are generally suggested meanings to dreams. I have said earlier in this book that only God can interpret dream. It is only to whom He releases the grace like He did unto Daniel and Joseph that can truly interpret a dream.

Although there are still men of God that has the grace to correctly interpret dreams, it is not all pastors who can accurately interpret or tell the meaning of every dream.

I have made attempts to highlight a few generally suggested meanings to some common things and symbols we often see in our dream, which often lead to destruction.

The meanings explained here are just to guide you the reader to have a general knowledge and know the kind of prayers to pray. It is to empower you to experience great deliverance and victory over destructive dreams.

I must also warn again that there may be other meanings to these dreams because many of these dreams are coded and come as parables.

A sister was once referred to me by a pastor friend. She had been pregnant fifteen times and suffered miscarriage after a certain dream. On some occasions, the baby died within five days.

She had the same dream continually where an elderly woman appears to her with a calabash and red palm oil. After this dream encounter, on that same day, she would have issue of blood and lose the pregnancy. She eventually relocated to USA; but the same thing continually re-occurred.

One can therefore conclude that, when this kind of from this situation persist, when people repeatedly have the same dream followed by and bad events, then demonic influence have stabilized their work in the life of such a person, and he or she therefore needs serious prayers of deliverance from the powers sponsoring destructive dreams.

DREAMS & GENERALLY ACCEPTED INTERPRETATIONS

1. **If you eat in the dream**
» It suggests that the enemy is trying to plant sickness or disease into your body

2. **If you are always sitting for examinations that you never finish**
» Disarrangement, stagnation, satanic delay and frustration

3. **If you find yourself drinking strong wine, beer or alcohol in the dream**
» Spirit of confusion and wastage

4. **When an unidentified person pursues you in the dream**
» A confused life and profitless hard work

5.   **If you see coffin or corpses in your dream**

»   Spirit of death is assigned against such a person

6.   **Having contacts with dead parents and relations**

»   It means there are ancestral covenants to be broken; and spiritual and physical illnesses planted in such a life

7.   **Attending funeral services frequently in the dream**

»   Spirit of death and pretence/deception by satanic agents are assigned against your life

8.   **If you see padlocks or doors locked with padlocks securely**

»   This means blessings are locked up

9.   **If you find yourself naked or half naked in the dream**

»   It signifies disgrace, shame and the loss of covering or one's glory; as well as insecurity

10.   **If you see dogs, snakes and birds attacking you in the dream**

»   Sickness and diseases are transferred by witchcraft power

11.   **If you find yourself in your old house, schools, former place of work**

»   It means backwardness, affliction, and poverty is planned by the enemy

12.   **If you are locked in a house with no window / door or any way of escape**

»   This is frustration and imprisonment

13.   If your feel heavy and pressed down in your sleep, or if a strange shadow oppresses you and which you can't resist
»   Satanic and witchcraft oppression

14.   If you see police or other uniform officers pursuing you for a possible arrest in your dream
»   Strange opposition against your destiny and fulfillment is arranged from the pit of hell

15.   If you see that you are hospitalized in a dream or bed- ridden or seriously injured in the dream
»   Sickness that may defy medication is planned against your life. You should seriously pray against this immediately

16.   Roaming about in the market
»   Financial recklessness and confusion is about to happen

17.   When you see dogs and they are friendly in your dream
»   Spirit of adultery or fornication is pursuing your life

18.   Having sexual intercourse in the dream
»   Spirit husband or wife afflicting your life

19.   If you see yourself in the midst of occultic people or members of secret cults or fraternity
»   Possible initiation arranged for you, and evil covenants must have been formed consciously or unconsciously with evil powers

20. **If you see masquerade in your dream**
» Deeply enchanted attack of satanic powers, deception, witchcraft attack, disgrace, restlessness is directed against you

21. **When you see thieves entering your house or you suffer burglary attack**
» This means spiritual attack and possible loss of precious possession and position

22. **When your marriage ring, dress or shoe is stolen; or your wedding gown turns into rag or is stained with blood or mud**
» There is an attack on your marital destiny

23. **Receiving gun shots in the dream**
» Satanic attack and witchcraft affliction

24. **If in a place of prayer you discover your Bible was stolen in the dream**
» This is loss of spiritual power; and attempt is been made to paralyze your spiritual life

25. **When you are travelling in a vehicle and it breaks down suddenly and there is no helper any where to fix it**
» Powers and principalities has been sponsored to arrest your prayers and delay your success and breakthrough in life

26. **If you see strong walls, obstacles or hindrances**
» Barriers are sponsored in your way. On-going projects become difficult to complete

27.   **When you see cobwebs in your dream or even on the road or all over your house, office, etc**
»   A very stubborn witchcraft attack with organized conspiracy from the pit of hell

28.   **If heavy loads are forced on your head in the dream**
»   Satanic and witchcraft transfer of problems by known person

29.   **Moving out of your matrimonial house in the dream**
»   Attack on your marriage designed to destroy your home

30.   **If you see fire suddenly explode in your house, office or known apartment/location**
»   Organized dangerous attack on your life is imminent

31.   **When the roof of a house is removed in the dream or the cap/crown on the head of an unknown figure or shadow is missing suddenly**
»   An arrow of sudden death is fired on the head of the family, mostly the husband

32.   **If you see blood from your own body in the dream either in your hand or on the ground or on any substance**
»   Your health is under serious attack by witchcraft powers

33.   **When a baby dies in your dream**
»   Your business or career is under attack. And witchcraft attack on your children must not be taken lightly

34.   **When a pregnant woman sees dead relation, cow, dog or masquerade/madman in her dream**
»   Spirit of death is on rampage against both the mother & baby. It is an attack of witches on the unborn baby. It is designed to generally terminate such a life before delivery. This is the spirit of Herod.

35.   **If you see dirty & stagnant waters in your dream**
»   This is the spirit of lukewarmness / discouragement.   It suggests lifting of the flesh over the spirit man

36.   **If you spend money lavishly; wear rags; walk on your feet; have leaking pockets; begging for alms; seeing rats and picking pockets**
»   Spirit of poverty is sponsored against your life and destiny

37.   **If you dream that you visit witch-doctors; take alcohol; or you see death or you are being buried**
»   Defeat in all your endeavourers and spiritual backwardness. Total destruction is the plan of the devil here.

38.   **When you see bats or other animals in the dream**
»   Difficulty, pretence, hypocrites, deceivers are preparing to enter your life

39.   **If a sister gets engaged to an unknown personality in the dream**

» The spirit of fornication and adultery has entered such life and confusion in marriage is planned by the enemy

40. **When you are abandoned in your dream**
» You will loose funds and vital relationships or a great investment. You must pray.

41. **If you see yourself with handcuffs in a dream**
» A power is placing a curse on your business or hardwork

42. **Climbing a mountain or ladder and unable to complete the exercise**
» Defeat and unprofitable labor

43. **If in your dream you discover that your hat was removed**
» It means an attack of your glory and honour. It suggests that your security is under threat from the forces of darkness

44. **If you see a great fire outburst in your dream**
» Danger is imminent

45. **If a strange woman or a shadow takes your husband away by force**
» Plans are on in the kingdom of the devil to snatch your husband

46. **If you see or receive a basket of flower or fruits as gift in the dream**
» Your breakthrough is about to come to manifestation (this is a good dream) and must

not be mistaken for destructive dream. Many people think it signifies burial of a dream. Pray for the manifestation of the good thing of life coming your way.

47.   If you see yourself taken away from a bigger chair or office or house to a smaller one
»   It signifies demotion and backwardness

48.   When a stranger claims ownership or take possession of what belongs to you, such as cars, house, land, etc.
»   Satanic obstacles and hindrances are always mounted against the project in your hand or your business

49.   If you find yourself doing very odd jobs
»   Disgrace, shame, ridicule and humiliation is sponsored against your destiny

50.   If you get married in the dream, give birth or carry out breast-feeding in the dream
»   It suggest barrenness, marital delays and draining of virtues of marital greatness

51.   If you appear before a judge in your dream with a police officer guiding you in handcuffs
»   Satanic judgment is about to be passed on the dreamer in the spirit world

52.   If you see evil marks, scratches or labels in your body or get infected in the dream
»   Spirit of rejection and hatred is sponsored by household witches. This is witchcraft identification mark

Suggested Prayers:

1.   Every good dream that I had dreamt shall manifest, in Jesus' name.

2.   My dream life shall not be hijacked by Satan, in Jesus' name.

3.   I receive power for positive dream in Jesus' name.

4.   Anointing for positive dreams fall upon me.

5.   My good dream will not fade out, in Jesus' name

6.   My memories shall be alive to my good dream, in Jesus' name.

7.   I shall receive angels of good news in my dreams, in Jesus' name

8.   I shall dream good dreams in Jesus' name

9.   I will not see lie in my dream, in Jesus' name.

10.   I receive grace for interpreting dreams, in Jesus' name.

CHAPTER SEVEN

Characteristics Of A Good Dream

It is common to associate certain dreams with evil. But you don't have to be afraid of every dream and their consequences.

Dreams usually evoke important thoughts and they lead to useful reflections. But whatever your dream may be, you have the power to make it comply with your own good. Don't let them bring only fear to you as it did to Elihpaz, the friend of Job. He said,

> *"Now a word was secretly brought to me, and my ear received a whisper of it. ^{13} In disquieting thoughts from the visions of the night, When deep sleep falls on men, ^{14} Fear came upon me, and trembling, which made all my bones shake" (Job 4: 12-14, NKJV)*

The activities you engage in during the day can trigger off a dream. A banker may see himself counting money in his dream. A footballer may see himself scoring goals, or an entertainer could see himself singing a song publicly.

You don't need to bother about such dreams. They are just a reflection of your state of mind.

> *" For a dream comes through much activity, And a fool's voice is known by his many words. [7] For in the multitude of dreams and many words there is also vanity. But fear God"* *(Eccl 5: 3, 7, NKJV)*

The emotionally state of a man greatly impacts on his dreams. The earnest expectations of a man's heart are usually replicated or imitated and replayed in his dreams. The Bible says,

> *"It shall even be as when an hungry man dreameth, and, behold, he eateth; but he awaketh, and his soul is empty: or as when a thirsty man dreameth, and, behold, he drinketh; but he awaketh, and, behold, he is faint, and his soul hath appetite: so shall the multitude of all the nations be, that fight against mount Zion"* *(Isa. 29: 8)*

As we have discussed earlier, there are indeed many dreams that convey good news and bring God's revelations to man.

We can also dream good dreams. But such dreams must be accompanied with or backed by very serious prayers to ensure the fulfillment of the blessings therein.

The Characteristics Of A Good Dream Include:

- If you receive basket of fruits, flowers in a dream, it suggest that blessings or good gifts are on the way

- If you see Jesus Christ or a renowned servant of God or an angel in your dream; it suggest that you are about receive a divine visitation

- If you see yourself in a farmland or by a field and the harvest is ripe and greenish; it suggest fulfilled result

- If you dream that chains are broken off your hands; it suggest a release for you.

But note that, every good dream must be prayed to reality or manifestation. Your earnest confession and prayer should be, **"My Good Dream Must Come To Pass, in Jesus' name!"**

Suggested Prayers:

"For surely there is an end; and thine expectation shall not be cut off" (Prov 23:18)

"For the vision is yet for an appointed time, but at the end it shall speak, and not lie: though it tarry, wait for it; because it will surely come, it will not tarry" (Habk 2:3)

1.	Every negative dream I ever had in my life, by the blood of Jesus be cancelled, in Jesus' name

2.	My Father, arise and send help to me in my dreams, in Jesus' name

3.	I receive the power to handle and enjoy the fruits of every good dream and vision I have had, in Jesus' name

4.	Every power manipulating my dreams, be disgraced, in Jesus' name

5.	Every good dream I ever had in the past come to pass by fire, in Jesus' name

6.	My dream of promotion, lifting, accomplishments, enjoyment, multiplication, come to fulfillment now, in Jesus' name

7.   Every power assigned against the fulfillment of my dream and vision be frustrated, in Jesus' name

8.   Every good vision and dream that people have seen concerning my life shall come to pass, in Jesus' name

9.   Power that delays the fulfillment of good dreams in my life, I command you to fail, in Jesus' name

10.   Household power sponsoring failure at the edge of my breakthroughs, fail in Jesus' name

11.   Every good dream of my life, begin to speak now, in Jesus' name

Chapter Eight

Signs of Destructive Dreams

There are some signals that can point a man to the fact that there are challenges or troubles ahead of him as a result of the kind of dream he often dreams.

This is very significant because dream, as we discussed earlier is a sort of spiritual bank of information.

The Bible explains that,

> *"... God may speak in one way, or in another, yet man does not perceive it. [15] In a dream, in a vision of the night, when deep sleep falls upon men, while slumbering on their beds, [16] Then He opens the ears of men, And seals their instruction. [17] In order to turn man from his deed, And conceal pride from man, [18] He keeps back his soul from the Pit, And his life from perishing by the sword"* (Job 33: 14-18)

From my counselling experience, I have discovered several indictors that are evident in dreams, which are destructive, and every effort must be made to destroy the satanic powers behind such dreams.

There are enough signals to show whether a dream is destructive or not. But **please note that, this is not to reduce dream interpretation to a formal standard.** The same thing can mean different things. We must therefore rely on the Holy Spirit

Dreams that have the following characteristics are destructive dreams:

- Always involving in climbing exercises in dreams and never getting to the top of the object.
- Sitting for examinations always in dreams without getting any result.
- Embarking on endless journeys.
- Consistent meaningless dreams that ends as nightmares.
- Always fighting unidentified person or persons without victory.
- Seeing dark rivers flowing always.
- Always plucking fruits from the tree, yet the fruits turn out to be rotten
- If you always serve people younger than you in your dreams
- When you always see yourself in a pit, prison, cell, or cage. It indicates stagnation.

- ➤ When you see rats running around you always
- ➤ Seeing yourself pregnant without delivering a baby
- ➤ If you are always going round in circles
- ➤ If you always wake up from the dream before something good happens or is about to happen in the dream.
- ➤ If you communicate with a dead person or relations regularly in your dreams.
- ➤ If you repeatedly have a terrible dream before a particular problem that occurs in your life.
- ➤ If you always receive a gift of a particular food items in your dream
- ➤ If you are cursed by an angry person in the dream.
- ➤ If you are harassed and pursued throughout in a dream.
- ➤ If you repeatedly find yourself in the graveyard.
- ➤ If you are looking for something in your dream and you are not able to locate it.
- ➤ If you get lost in a forest.
- ➤ If you consistently fight with giants in your dream.
- ➤ If you are locked out or denied access, while others are allowed in.
- ➤ If you find yourself crying in the dream without any reason.
- ➤ If you are always fighting invisible shadows in the dream
- ➤ When you always find barriers on your journey or way

- ➢ If always encounter evil occurrences in your dreams.
- ➢ If you are always robbed.
- ➢ If you always fall at the peak of a ladder.
- ➢ If you see a friend suddenly become an enemy in your dream.
- ➢ When you are always naked or raped
- ➢ If you always wear one leg of shoe in the dream
- ➢ When masquerade or unidentified person appear often in your dream
- ➢ If you repeatedly find yourself in positions or classes you have passed out of earlier in life.

SOME OBSERVATIONS ABOUT DESTRUCTIVE DREAMS

It has been observed that people who have such dreams often experience the following in their lives:

- Sickness and unexplainable death.
- Trials and temptations.
- Accident and incurable diseases.
- Anger and bitterness, unforgiveness and confusion.
- Failures at the edge of miracles.
- Such people rarely get helpers.
- They cannot complete meaningful projects in life.
- Friends suddenly become enemies.
- Stagnated life and backwardness.

- They are always frustrated, disgraced and suffer rejection.
- They get robbed of blessings and promotions.
- They unintentionally and inexplicably offend their helpers.
- They always face barriers and obstacles in life.
- They toil and struggle, yet without any corresponding result.
- They fight invisible shadows

Suggested Prayers:

1.   Signs and wonders that I see in my dream shall blossom greatly in Jesus' name

2.   Fearful, attacking dreams and nightmares; be cancelled out of my life, in Jesus' name.

3.   Destructive dreams planned to destroy me, be destroyed, in Jesus' name.

4.   Every satanic dream dreamt about me by anyone; be cancelled, in Jesus' name.

5.   Threats of death, sickness and attack in my dream, I reject you in Jesus' name.

6.   My Father, reveal your mind to me in my dreams tonight, in Jesus' name.

7.   Every satanic attempt to deceive me in my dreams, be frustrated, in Jesus' name.

8.   Blood of Jesus erase all my evil dreams

9.   Heavenly Father, arise and set my destiny free in Jesus' name.

10.   Every power of my father's house, hunting for my life, die in Jesus' name

## CHAPTER NINE

Handling Destructive Dreams

Destructive dreams are avenues through which the devil and forces of darkness afflict so many people and their destinies.

Even though man is destined to dream dreams, many people cannot handle destructive dreams and contend with their evils and overcome them.

Yet, we have the ability to tackle such dreams and stop their evil plans.

The following simple steps would readily help you to win the battles over destructive dreams:

1.   Be Born Again:
This qualifies you to receive the power to become the child of God, whosoever abide under the shadow of the Almighty, enjoys the covenant of divine protection.

2.	Live Holy:
Holiness is what will guarantee the presence of God with you, to drive away satanic attacks. On the other hand, sin opens you up for the oppression of the enemy as it breaks God's protective shield over your life. Remember that, *"he that digs a pit, the serpent shall bite"*.

3.	Live By The Word of God:
Read and study your Bible and meditate upon the Word of God always.

The Word of God gives sufficient light to quench or douse the evils of darkness. The Word will guide and strengthen you even in the face of destructive dreams; because it reveals the mind of God to you.

4.	Be Baptised in The Holy Spirit:
This is clear and simple.

Without the power of the Holy Spirit, you cannot achieve anything in life, let alone be able to understand your dreams or even stand against the enemies of your life.

If you are baptised in the Holy Ghost, you become a fire-brand Christian whom the enemy cannot toy with.

5.	Have Faith in The Word of God:
Usually, the attacks of the enemy against our lives begin with their spoken words or evil pronouncements, and destructive dreams are one of

the veritable ways their evils are projected into people's lives
.

But the Word of God says, *"Ye are of God, little children, and have overcome them: because greater is he that is in you, than he that is in the world" (1 John 4: 4).*

The Word of God also says, *"No weapon that is formed against thee shall prosper; and every tongue that shall rise against thee in judgment thou shalt condemn. This is the heritage of the servants of the LORD, and their righteousness is of me, saith the LORD" (Isa. 54:17)*

Indeed, the enemy would send his evil dreams; but as a child of God, you must hold onto the Word of God, and declare its truth and the enemy would flee from you. There is power in the Word of God.

6.   Cast Out Fear, Worry And Anxiety

What the enemy does or attempts to do through his destructive dreams is to cause you to fear, and once you become fearful, your faith in God becomes shaken. This exposes you to his attacks and oppression.

But if you stand your grounds and resist the enemy, you would discover that fear, worries and unnecessary anxieties which gladden the enemy can easily be overcome.

Remember too that without faith we cannot please God; and if our ways pleases the Lord, he makes even our enemies, seen and unseen to be at peace with us.

7.   Avoid Bad Association:
The people you associate with go a long way to determine, shape or influence your life, either positively or negatively.

Evil and wrong company would only bring evil results. And since a lot of dreams come as a result of people's real life experiences, your daily life encounter is partly transferred or re-played in your dream life. And if such encounters are wrong, then the result is obvious.

Please know that the devil can comprehensively have access to your life and destiny through the company or people you associate with.

8.   Be Careful of The Food You Eat:
A lot of food people eat, has the ability to weaken the spirit or soul of man. Food props up the flesh, and as the flesh is elevated, the spirit is subdued.

This is why when people eat excessively, they tend to dream, and such dreams are usually negative.

9.   Be Prayerful:
Prayer is the number one key to overcoming any plan of the enemy including destructive dreams.

When we pray, we call upon God to intervene in our affairs; and once God rises on our behalf, no one can be against us.

The Bible says, *"For we do not wrestle against flesh and blood, but against principalities, against powers, against the rulers of the darkness of this age, against spiritual hosts of wickedness in the heavenly places" (Eph 6:12)* and the power we have over them is embedded in our prayers.

The Bible also says, *"For the weapons of our warfare are not carnal but mighty in God for pulling down strongholds, [5] casting down arguments and every high thing that exalts itself against the knowledge of God, bringing every thought into captivity to the obedience of Christ" (2 Cor 10:4)*

Destructive dreams are also strong fortification of evil which are to be battered down and laid in ruins by our spiritual weapons and prayers empowered by God.

As the enemy wishes you evil through dreams, may your prayers pull down their plans and turn around their evils for good, in Jesus' name!

A 3 DAY PRAYER PROGRAMME TO OVERCOME DESTRUCTIVE DREAMS

Whenever you have a destructive dream, I recommend you pray the prayers suggested here for three days, and I trust the God that answers prayers would turn around every evil of the enemy against your life, in Jesus' name.

Note:

- Plead the Blood of Jesus (Rev 12:11, Exo 12:13). The blood of Jesus is a potential weapon against destructive dreams. Destructive dreams be canceled by the blood of Jesus

- Challenge those dreams with the name of Jesus Christ, the name that is above all names (Phil 2: 9-10, Prov 18:10)

- Employ the Fire of God (Isa 66:15)

- Engage the angels of God to fight for you (Ps 91:10-11, Ps 35:4-6). Command the angels to deal with destructive dreams. They are ministering spirits.

Destructive dreams be canceled by the blood of Jesus

DAY ONE:

CONFESSION:
"Who hath delivered us from the power of darkness, and hath translated us into the kingdom of his dear Son: 14 In whom we have redemption through his blood, even the forgiveness of sins" (Col 1: 13-14)

1.   Every cloud of darkness covering/removing my destiny, be disgraced, in Jesus' name.

2.   My Father, make your ways plain before me, in Jesus' name.

3.   Every power assigned against my destiny at the edge of miracle, be disgraced, in Jesus' name.

4.   Holy Spirit, terminate every unprofitable labour in my life, in Jesus' name.

5.   Every power strengthening the ladder of poverty in my life, be frustrated, in Jesus' name.

6.   Ungodly delays and discouragements, be disgraced out of my life, in Jesus' name.

7.   Every dream of defeat, poverty and backsliding, fail now, in Jesus' name.

8.   You satanic basket of the enemy on my head, catch fire, in Jesus' name.

9.   Every spirit troubling my life I challenge you by the blood of Jesus. Depart from my life now, in Jesus' name.

10.   Dreams of poverty, diseases and affliction, I cast you out in Jesus name

11.   My Father, by your power, remove me from the school of confusion, in Jesus' name.

12.   Spirit of abandonment depart from my life permanently, in Jesus' name.

13.   Satanic animals assigned against my life, die by fire, in Jesus' name.

14.   Arrows of confusion and manipulation in my dreams, go back to sender, in Jesus' name.

15.   Spirit of abandonment, depart by fire, in Jesus' name.

16.   Every ancestral covenants between myself and divine relocation, break in Jesus' name

17.   Fire of God, arise and destroy all evil armies assigned against my destiny, in Jesus' name.

18.   My Father, arise, and heal my wounds, in Jesus' name.

19.   I command every satanic handcuffs in my dream, catch fire, in Jesus' name.

20.   Every satanic mountain standing as a stumbling block to my victory, be destroyed, in Jesus' name.

21.   Every plan of the enemy to put me to shame, be disgraced, in Jesus' name.

22.   Every dirty water polluting my life through my dream, dry up now., in Jesus' name.

23.   Angels of God, repair the vehicle of my destiny, in Jesus' name.

24.   Spirit of uncertainty, confusion and stagnation, depart away from my life, in Jesus' name.

25.   Satanic handwriting against my destiny, be nullified, in Jesus' name.

26.   Every opposition in my dream, become victory, in Jesus' name.

27.   Every attempt of the enemy to deceive me in my dream shall fail woefully, in Jesus' name.

28.   I command every scar in my dream to become stars, in Jesus' name.

29.   Oh Lord, turn every failure to success, trails to triumph, tests to testimonies, bondage to foundation, losses to gain, and weaknesses to strength, in Jesus' name

30.   Every eating and drinking of spiritual poison in my dream, end today, in Jesus' name.

31.   Destruction, demoting and devastating dreams be nullified out of my life, in Jesus' name.

32.   Satanic broadcaster of my destiny in the dreams, be silenced, in Jesus' name.

33.   My Father, anoint me for victory in my dream daily, in Jesus' name.

34.   Stubborn pursuers of my destiny attacking me in night dream, die by fire, in Jesus' name.

35.   Oh Lord trouble my troublers in the dream, in Jesus' name.

36.   Every animal or bird sent to me in my dreams, return to sender, in Jesus' name.

DAY TWO:

CONFESSION:

"He that dwelleth in the secret place of the most High shall abide under the shadow of the Almighty.
[2] I will say of the LORD, He is my refuge and my fortress: my God; in him will I trust.
[3] Surely he shall deliver thee from the snare of the fowler, and from the noisome pestilence.
[4] He shall cover thee with his feathers, and under his wings shalt thou trust: his truth shall be thy shield and buckler.
[5] Thou shalt not be afraid for the terror by night; nor for the arrow that flieth by day;
[6] Nor for the pestilence that walketh in darkness; nor for the destruction that wasteth at noonday"
(Psalm 91: 1-6)

1.   My father, let all my good dreams come to pass

2.   All evil dreams, be replaced with the blessings of God that adds no sorrow

3.   Blood of Jesus arise, nullify all destructive dreams and their effects upon my life

4.   Every sickness planted in my body through destructive dreams, blood of Jesus, remove them

5.   Every night creature, sponsored against my dream life, die

6.   Every coffin prepared for me and my family in the dream, catch fire

7.   Every plantation in my body come out by fire

8.   Satanic dream, get out and be replaced with heavenly visions of greatness and prosperity in Jesus name.

9.   Power and principalities sponsoring bad dreams into my life be disgraced, in Jesus' name.

10.   Satanic covenants and initiation in my dream, be cancelled by the blood of Jesus

11.   My Father, convert every trial in my dream to triumph, failure to success and scars to stars, in Jesus' name.

12.   Satanic manipulation through my dreams be cancelled by the blood of Jesus, in Jesus' name.

13.   Satanic spiritual loads placed on my head in my dream catch fire, in Jesus' name.

14.   Arrows of sudden death in my dream, return to sender, in Jesus' name.

15.   Satanic calendar assigned against my life catch fire, in Jesus' name.

16.   Oh Lord destroy the seed of the enemy in my life, in Jesus' name.

17.   Satanic animals prepared to attack me in the night, die by fire, in Jesus' name.

18.   Every cats, dogs, rat, ant, beast, cow, snake, lizards, snails, vultures tormenting my life, die now, in Jesus' name.

19.   Satanic manipulation in my dream, be nullified, in Jesus' name.

20.	My good dreams, vision, begin to manifest by fire, in Jesus' name.

21.	Every mountain standing before me and my good dream become plain, in Jesus' name.

22.	Let my dream of breakthrough, accomplishment, promotion, advancement, manifest by fire, in Jesus' name.

23.	My Father, close the gap between my journey into greatness and its fulfillment, in Jesus' name.

24.	Arrows of delay, distraction, stagnation go back to sender, in Jesus' name.

25.	Arrows of wastage, defeat, barrenness, go back to sender, in Jesus' name.

26.	My Father arise and put an end to sexual intimacy in my dream; and let eating, drinking, slavery, nakedness, depart by fire, in Jesus' name.

27.	Strange activities assigned against my home in the dream be scattered, in Jesus' name.

28.	Every satanic verdict passed against me in my dream by reversed, in Jesus' name.

29.	Satanic identification marks upon my life and destiny, be cancelled by the blood of Jesus

30.	My Father, arise strengthen my ladder of greatness, in Jesus' name.

31.	Powers of disgrace assigned against my destiny be frustrated, in Jesus' name.

32.	Vagabond spirit prepared against my life in the dream, be disgraced, in Jesus' name.

33.   Satanic traps prepared for my life, begin to catch fire now, in Jesus' name.

34.   Every benefits, breakthrough and goodness stolen from me in the dream, I receive you back by fire, in Jesus' name.

35.   Power of the night fashioned against my life, die by fire, in Jesus' name.

36.   Every good thing I have lost in my dream from birth, I recover by fire, in Jesus' name.

37.   I reject every form of witchcraft incitation in the dream, in Jesus' name.

DAY THREE:

CONFESSION:
"You shall not be afraid of the terror by night, Nor of the arrow that flies by day,
⁶ Nor of the pestilence that walks in darkness, Nor of the destruction that lays waste at noonday"
(Ps 91: 5-6).

1.   I shall have great understanding in dreams, in Jesus' name.

2.   I reject every false dream that is working against me in the physical, in Jesus' name

3.   Grace to remember my dream, fall upon me, in

4.	I am delivered from the hands of dream killers, in Jesus' name.

5.	I will not suffer many evil things because of my dreams, in Jesus' name

6	My dreams shall not be used against me in Jesus name, in Jesus' name

7.	Powers of the night manipulating my dream life be disgraced, in Jesus' name.

8.	All evil dreams in my life, by the blood of Jesus, be cancelled, in Jesus' name.

9.	Dreams of destruction, stop in my life, and be destroyed, in Jesus' name.

10	Every power assigned to plant sickness in my life through my dream, be destroyed, in Jesus' name.

11.	Arrows of sudden death fired into my life in my dream go out by fire; in Jesus' name.

12.	Oh Lord, my God, my Father, arise fight for me in my dream, in Jesus' name.

13.	Almighty Father, arise, fight for me and deliver me from every witchcraft dream, in Jesus' name.

14.	Blood of Jesus, cancel every evil dream assigned to stop my prosperity, in Jesus' name.

15.   Every friendly Judas manifesting in my dream life, be exposed and disgraced, in Jesus' name.

16.   Every activity of familiar spirit in my dreams be frustrated, in Jesus' name.

17.   Satanic canteens; satanic hands severing me evil and contaminated food in my dreams, catch fire, in Jesus' name.

18.   Anything planted in my life that is contrary to the will of God be uprooted by fire, in Jesus' name.

19.   Every power attacking my marriage in my dream, die, in Jesus' name.

20.   Satanic animals assigned to hurt me in my dream be roasted by fire, in Jesus' name.

21.   Every killer devil assigned to destroy me in the dreams, catch fire, in Jesus' name.

22.   Every pot calling my name for destruction, scatter in Jesus' name.

23.   By the blood of Jesus Christ, I stand against evil dream, in Jesus' name.
24.   Demonic attacks in my dream, stop, in Jesus' name.

25.   Every satanic covenant and initiation through dreams affecting my life negatively, break now, in Jesus' name.

26.   Every defeat in my dreams, become victory, in Jesus' name.

27.   Powers of darkness and principalities assigned against my dream life, fail and fall flat, in Jesus' name.

28.   I recover by fire all my stolen virtues, blessing, etc, in Jesus' name

29.   Satanic animal appearing in my dream, die, in Jesus' name.

30.   You powers polluting dreams, release me now, in Jesus' name.

31.   Let my family receive deliverance by fire, in Jesus' name.

32.   Every power assigned to destroy my family, die, in Jesus' name.

33.   By the blood of Jesus, I recover all my stolen blessings in my dreams, in Jesus' name.

Your Salvation is The Key To Breakthrough

I must emphasis here that it is not every prayer that God hears or answers. If you are not born again, you cannot have any access to God through prayers.

It is a person's status as a child of God that qualifies him or her to receive God's attention. But you can get God to turn His face to you if you want to pray the prayer of salvation. This is the key that would open every other door of blessing.

If you want to accept the Lord Jesus Christ as your Lord and personal Saviour right now and qualify to receive all the grace and glory God has promised, then read aloud and confess the following simple prayer and accept it as true.

Dear Heavenly Father, in response to your word, I come to you in the name of Jesus -for a new beginning.

I pray and ask Jesus to come into my heart and be the Lord over my life. And I give you all the glory.

I believe and confess that Jesus Christ is the Son of God and the Lord. I believe that He was raised from the dead for my justification. According to your word *"...with the heart man believeth unto righteousness..."* and I do believe with my heart, I am now a child of God. I am saved.

Praise the Lord.

<u>BIBLIOGRAPHY</u>

1.   Longman Dictionary Of Contemporary English.

2.   The World Book Energy Encyclopaedia 1995
        World Book Inc.

3.   The Holy Bible KJV.

Other Books By Samuel A. Wright

As a child of God, you need to understand the mystery of the night to be able to overcome the attacks and wiles of the devil and his cohorts.

This book will give you an insight into the operations of the evil ones at night and it offers keys to overcome every of their evil plans against you and your destiny.

"The Pains of Unforgiveness":

No matter how great you are, unforgiveness will turn God against you and ultimately destroy your life and destiny.

This book exposes the truth, dangers and pains you suffer for being unforgiving, and it offers steps to help you live as God wants you to live.

It is a must-read for every Christian who wants to live victoriously as true Kingdom citizens.

Other Books By Samuel A. Wright

This book gives a concise insight into the tremendous power and truth of divine healing. You will find simple keys to receive miraculous healing and how to walk in the grace of sound health.

If you have even been bothered about divine healing- when, where and how it will happen for you - then you need to read this book.

The blessings of God comes with conditions.

This book highlights the steps of Abraham that led to his enduring prosperity. It will help and guide you to receive God's ultimate blessings, and expose some "Faith Pits" you must avoid in the journey of life.

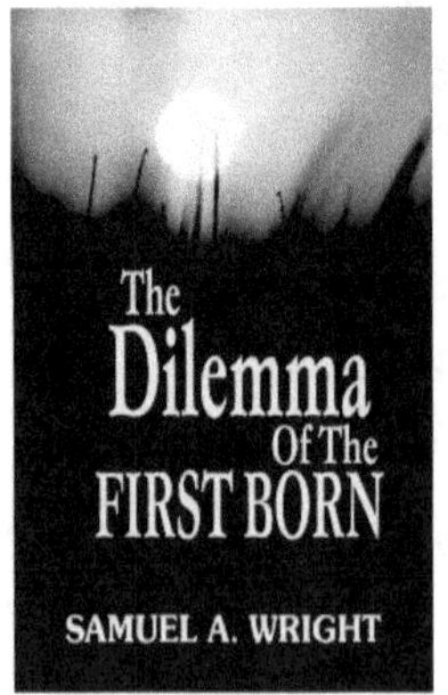

The Dilemma of The First Born
It is great to be a first born. The first born always bring joy to the family.
But in spite of the many benefits that come with being a first born, there are numerous challenges, responsibilities, even attacks that rage against the first born in families.
If you are a first born or you have a first born, then you need to read this book!

Other Books By Samuel A. Wright

"Bible Pattern For Choosing a life Partner":
God ordained marriage to be enjoyed. But marriage can only be a blessing if you have the right spouse.
This book will give you necessary biblical tips in making the right choice to make your marriage conform to God's plan from the foundation.
If you are planning to get married, you need to read this book before you make that decision.

Disgracing The Spirit of Rejection
When you are rejected and cast away by those you love, by those who once swore to love you, by friends and associates, what do you do?
Rejection drives people to frustration, low-self esteem, and it causes many emotional disorders that are feuled by evil forces to destroy peoples destiny. This book will help you win the battle against those forces.

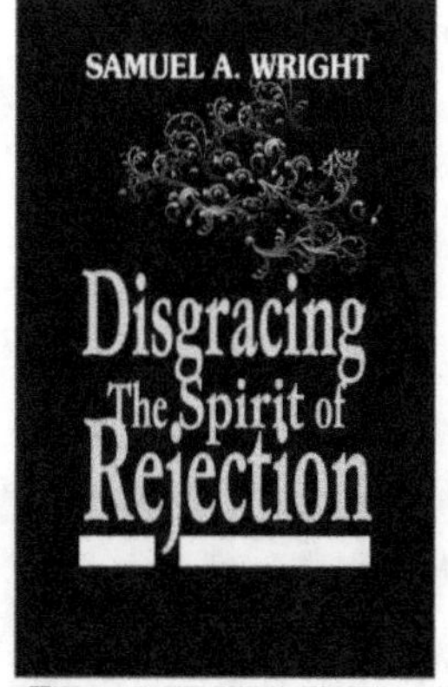

My Pastor & I
This is perhaps the most incisive book that reveals and addresses issues to help you overcome misconceptions about your relationship with your pastor. It would help you build a lasting and fruitful relationship with your pastor and position you to enjoy the best of God in the church. If you have a pastor in your church and you desire to be truly functional in the body of Christ, then you must read this book!

Other Books By Samuel A. Wright

Innocent But Guilty!

Have you even been accused falsely, yet you can't prove your innocence? Have you been betrayed by those you love?

When you don't have an answer to the accusations of the enemy, what do you do? This book gives biblical insights and tips to handling such situations. It is a must read!

"Covenant Demand For Divine Protection":

As a child of God, you are under a covenant of protection. But you have a role to play to enjoy this grace.

This book will guide you on that path and make you become untouchable to the enemy.

Let Us Pray!

Indeed there is power in prayer and praying. But you would discovered that there are several people who pray yet get no answers. Are you in this category? This book highlights the many hindrances to answered prayers, and it offers keys to make prayers a rewarding exercise for you.

Pastor Samuel Abiodun Wright is dynamic preacher and teacher whose mesage of hope and restoration have imparted many souls both at local and international conferences and conventions.

He is the Senior Pastor of the fast growing Redeeming Hope Christian Centre with branches in different parts of Nigeria, Ghana, South Africa and a thriving outreach in India. He is also the president of Alpha Mission International, Ogun State, Nigeria.

Wright holds degrees in English Language and Religious Education. He also obtained a Diploma in Theology, a PGD in Missions and a Leadership Diploma Certificate from WOFBI, Lagos, Nigeria.

He is an Alumnus of the United Christian Church and Ministerial Association, USA and the Haggai Institute for Leadership and Advanced Training, Singapore.

He is married to Oluyimika and they are blessed with children.

For more information or enquiries;
or if this book has touched and impacted
your life, and you want to share your
testimony with us, to the glory of God,
please contact:

Redeeming Hope Christian Centre
14, Water Pipeline Road, Baale-Ajuwon,
Akute, Ogun State, Nigeria.
P. O. Box 11966, Ikeja, Lagos, Nigeria.
Tel: 234 - 01- 472 4219, 234- 802 321 3827
e-mail: alpha1_ministries@yahoo.com
www.redeeminghopechristiancenter.org

9 789785 015133